Gi

MW01277265

# Birthday Party Bedlam

Jacqueline Arena

illustrated by

Lloyd Foye

MACMILLAN

First published in 2008 by
MACMILLAN EDUCATION AUSTRALIA PTY LTD
15–19 Claremont Street, South Yarra 3141

Visit our website at www.macmillan.com.au or
go directly to www.macmillanlibrary.com.au

Associated companies and representatives throughout the world.



National Library of Australia
Cataloguing-in-Publication data

Arena, Jacqueline.
Birthday party bedlam.

For primary school students.
ISBN 978 1 4202 6146 2 (pbk.).
ISBN 978 1420262179 (set 3)

1. Birthday parties – Juvenile fiction. I. Title. (Series: Girlz rock!).

A 823.4

Series created by Felice Arena and Phil Kettle
Project management by Limelight Publishing Services Pty Ltd
Cover and text design by Lore Foye
Illustrations by Lloyd Foye

Printed in China

GIRLZ ROCK!

# Contents


CHAPTER 1
**Are You Crazy?** **1**

CHAPTER 2
**Pin Another Nose** **7**

CHAPTER 3
**Splash!** **13**

CHAPTER 4
**Ready, Set, GO!** **20**

CHAPTER 5
**Balloon Trouble** **26**

**EXTRA STUFF**

- Birthday Party Lingo 33
- Birthday Party Must-dos 34
- Birthday Party Instant Info 36
- Think Tank 38
- Hey Girls! (Author Letter) 40
- When We Were Kids 42
- What a Laugh! 43

Rachel Ellie

CHAPTER 1

# Are You Crazy?

Best friends Rachel and Ellie are talking about Rachel's little cousin's birthday party.

**Ellie** "So, let me get this right. You told your mum that you would help plan and run your little cousin's birthday party—tomorrow?"

**Rachel** "Yep!"

**Ellie** "And that I would help you?"

**Rachel** "Yep!"

**Ellie** "Ten five-year-old boys running all over the place?"

**Rachel** "Yep!"

**Ellie** "Rach, are you crazy? They're going to eat us alive. That's like being thrown into the lion's den or something."

**Rachel** "El, don't flip out. I have it under control. Remember at our school class party? I was one of the main helpers."

**Ellie** "How could I forget? You were like a sergeant in the army. You ordered everyone to dance the chicken dance, even Mr. Jones! And he hates to dance."

**Rachel** "Yeah, well I'm glad I did, because it would've been boring as! So, what party game should we start with?"

**Ellie** "I don't know ... um, what about Pin the Tail on the Donkey."

**Rachel** "Yeah, good idea."

Rachel runs off into the other room and returns a few minutes later with cardboard, paper, pens, scissors and a blindfold.

**Ellie** "What's all this?"

**Rachel** "Start drawing a donkey, El. I'll draw a tail and cut it out. Then we'll try it out."

**Ellie** "Why do we have to try it out?"

**Rachel** "Because we have to have a practice run of all the games. You can never be too ready. Now start drawing!"

Ellie stands up and salutes Rachel as if she's an officer in the army.

**Ellie** "Sir! Yes, sir!"

**Rachel** "Ha, ha! Very funny."

## CHAPTER 2

# Pin Another Nose

Rachel hangs up Ellie's picture of a donkey on the living room wall.

**Rachel** "Um, nice pic, El."

**Ellie** "You think? It looks more like an anteater than a donkey."

**Rachel** "Yeah, and my cut-out tail looks more like a nose."

**Ellie** "Then let's call it Pin Another Nose on the Anteater."

**Rachel** "Yes! That's cool! Right. Now put this blindfold on and try it."

**Ellie** "Why do I have to do it?"

**Rachel** "Because I'm in charge."
**Ellie** "Oh, yeah, how could I forget?"

Rachel ties the blindfold around Ellie's face, places the cut-out nose in her hand, spins her around a couple of times and points her in the direction of the anteater.

**Rachel** "Okay, go for it, El."

**Ellie** "I'm dizzy."

**Rachel** "That's it. You're only a few steps away."

**Ellie** "You know I didn't really need a blindfold. I could've just taken my glasses off. I can't see a thing without them."

**Rachel** "Stop talking, El. You're almost there."

**Ellie** "You know, I'm helping you, and all you're doing is being bossy."

**Rachel** "Sorry."

*Ding dong!* The doorbell rings and Rachel goes to see who it is. When she returns, she is shocked to see that Ellie has missed the picture completely and is walking straight towards a vase filled with flowers.

**Rachel** "El, what are you doing? The anteater is behind you! Stop! Don't move!"

**Ellie** "What?"

But it's too late. Ellie knocks over the vase.

CHAPTER 3

# Splash!

Rachel's mother comes rushing in to find the vase in pieces. Ellie says she's sorry. Rachel's mother tells her not to worry. She says it was an old vase, but suggests that Ellie and Rachel continue their party planning outside.

**Ellie** "I feel so bad. Why didn't you stop me?"

**Rachel** "I tried. Don't stress. Mum said it's okay."

**Ellie** "Well, maybe you shouldn't have that game for your cousin's party."

**Rachel** "Yeah, maybe you're right. But I've got a better party game we can play."

**Ellie** "What?"

**Rachel** "Bobbing for apples."

Rachel runs off and gets a bucket and fills it with water. She drops five apples in it.

**Rachel** "Right. You have to put your hands behind your back, get on your knees and try to scoop out the apples with your mouth. Each person gets two minutes, and the person who has taken out the most apples in that time wins."

**Ellie** "That sounds like fun."

**Rachel** "And we can both try this one."

Rachel and Ellie take turns bobbing their faces into the bucket, giggling as they try to bite at the apples. Suddenly, Rachel's brother appears and dunks their heads deep into the bucket and runs off.

**Rachel** "Arrgghh! You're gonna pay for that!"

**Ellie** "Where are my glasses? I hope he didn't step on them."

**Rachel** "Come back here, coward."

Rachel tosses the bucket of water at her brother just as her mother steps outside the house to see what's going on. Rachel misses her brother and drenches her mother instead.

**Rachel** "Oh, no!"
**Ellie** "Found 'em!"

CHAPTER 4

# Ready, Set, GO!

Rachel and Ellie are sitting on swings in the backyard.

**Ellie** "I've never seen your mum so mad before."

**Rachel** "Yeah, I know."

**Ellie** "She was so mad. Her face was all squished up, and for a moment there I thought I saw horns coming out of her head."

**Rachel** "Yeah, well it was my brother's fault. He's a rat."

**Ellie** "So, what are we going to do now?"

**Rachel** "We have a party to plan and run."

**Ellie** "Do you mean run or ruin?"

**Rachel** "What?"

**Ellie** "Nothing."

**Rachel** "I've got it!"

**Ellie** "Got what?"

**Rachel** "Another party game idea."

**Ellie** "I don't like the sound of this."

Rachel hops off the swing and runs over to the garden shed at the back of the yard. She returns to Ellie a few moments later with two potato sacks in her hand.

**Ellie** "What are they for?"

**Rachel** "For sack racing. It's a favourite at birthday parties. My cousin and his friends will love this one. Come on! I'll race ya."

The girls run to the back of the yard and hop into their sacks.

**Rachel** “Okay, first one up to the vegie patch wins. Ready, set, GO!”

**Ellie** "This is cool! I'm going to totally win this one."

With only centimetres to go, the girls trip over each other and fall on top of the vegie patch—squashing Rachel's mother's tomatoes.

**Rachel** "Oh no! We're in big trouble."

CHAPTER 5

# Balloon Trouble

Rachel's mother is furious with the girls for squashing her tomatoes. She sends them to Rachel's bedroom.

**Ellie** "Okay, when I said I've never seen your mum so mad before, I was wrong. Now *that* was mad. It was like a wizard had turned her into a dragon. For a moment there, I thought I saw flames coming out of her mouth."

**Rachel** "Well, she does love her tomatoes."

**Ellie** "So, now what are we going to do?"

**Rachel** "You can help me blow up these balloons."

**Ellie** "You still want to do this?"

**Rachel** "Yeah."

**Ellie** "After all we've been through? Planning your little cousin's birthday party has been more trouble than it's worth. It's been complete birthday party bedlam."

**Rachel** "I know. But how hard is it to blow up balloons?"

Rachel and Ellie begin to blow up balloons.

**Rachel** "There. We're done. And nothing happened."

Suddenly, a huge gust of wind gushes through Rachel's bedroom window and blows some of the balloons outside.

**Ellie** "Rach, the balloons!"

**Rachel** "Look! They're going into the yard next door."

**Ellie** "Oh no! Now they're going into your neighbours' pool."

**Rachel** "I don't believe it! You're right, El. This sucks!"

Rachel's mother enters Rachel's room after seeing the balloons float past the kitchen window. She offers to plan the birthday party and suggests that perhaps Rachel could help prepare some birthday food instead.

**Rachel** "That's a great idea, Mum. I'll make cupcakes. The best cupcakes ever. And El can help me."

**Ellie** (rolling her eyes) "Here we go again."

Rachel

GIRLZROCK!

# Birthday Party Lingo

Ellie

**bobbing** When you dip your head up and down—especially when you're trying to get apples out of a bucket filled with water.

**cake** Mmmm! We all know what cake means! I WANT CAKE NOW!!

**candles** The best things to stick into your birthday cake, apart from your mouth.

**happy** The way you'll feel when you have a party with your friends—and when you open up all your birthday presents.

**music** It's on your favourite CD, and it's what you should play loudly at your party.

GIRLZROCK!

# Birthday Party Must-dos

☆ Have a cake. That's the most important thing to have at a birthday party. Everyone loves cake. And besides, where else are you going to stick your candles?

☆ Blow out the candles on your birthday cake and make a wish, but don't tell anyone, or it won't come true.

☆ Always be gracious when accepting gifts. Saying, "Oh, is this all you got me?" is not a good look. Never expect gifts. The greatest gift is having all your friends around you, having a good time. Yeah, right. Who am I kidding? BRING ON THE PRESENTS!

☆ Sing "Happy Birthday to You" at the top of your voice, even if it's off key. You're allowed to, it's your birthday.

☆ Play plenty of music—all your favourite music—not your mum's and dad's, unless their favourites are your favourites, too.

☆ Have games. Plenty of them. If your friends get bored, move on to the next game. If you run out of games, get your friends to help you annoy your brother, or … have more cake!

☆ Help clean up after your birthday party has ended. The best way to do this is to tell your parents you think your brother should help. After all, it is your special day!

# Birthday Party Instant Info

- People in Australia and England who celebrate their one hundredth birthday receive a birthday message from the Queen.
- Harry Potter's birthday is 31 July. It's also J.K. Rowling's birthday.
- "Happy Birthday to You" is the most sung melody in the world. We usually sing it when a cake is brought out to the person celebrating their birthday.
- In Australia, when you have your eighteenth birthday you are allowed to vote in government elections.

- The most common birthday in America is 5 October and the least common is 22 May.

- To say "Happy Birthday!" in Italian, you'd say, "Buon Compleanno!". In French it's "Joyeux Anniversaire!" and in Chinese Mandarin it's "qu ni sheng er kuai le!".

GirlzRock!

# Think Tank

1 Pin the Tail on the Donkey is often played at birthday parties. True or False?

2 What's the number one food item you should have at a birthday party?

3 How many candles do you need if you are celebrating your ninth birthday?

4 What song does everyone sing at your birthday party?

5 Who gets the presents if you're celebrating a birthday?

6 Your birthday means the day you first went to school. True or False?

7 Who are the best people to celebrate your birthday with?

8 What should you do when you blow out the candles on your birthday cake?

## Answers

1 True. But it's a game you can play anytime.

2 The number one food item you should have is CAKE!!!

3 If it's your ninth birthday, you need nine candles, of course!

4 Everyone at a birthday party sings "Happy Birthday to You".

5 You! You get all those presents. It's your birthday.

6 False. Your birthday is the anniversary of the day you were born—"birth" + "day". Get it?

7 The best people to celebrate your birthday with are your friends and family.

8 When you blow out the candles on your cake, you make a wish.

## How did you score?

- If you got all 8 answers correct, you absolutely love birthday parties. You know exactly how many more sleeps until your next birthday.
- If you got 6 answers correct, then you love to be invited to birthday parties and love the games and party gift packs.
- If you got fewer than 4 answers correct, you have trouble remembering your friends' birthdays. Sometimes you forget your own!

Hey Girls!

I hope that you have as much fun reading my story as I have had writing it. I loved reading and writing stories when I was growing up—I still do!

Here are some suggestions that might help you enjoy reading even more than you do now. At school, why don't you use "Birthday Party Bedlam" as a play? And you and your friends can be the actors. Get some streamers and some balloons, and make your own Pin the Tail on the Donkey game. Use these as props.

So ... have you decided who is going to be Rachel and who is going to be Ellie? And what about the narrator?

*Now act out the story in front of your friends ... you'll have a great time! You also might like to take this story home and get someone in your family to read it with you. Maybe they can take on a part in the story.*

*Whatever you choose to do, remember, reading and writing is a whole lot of fun ... and girls totally rock!*

*Take care,*

Jacqueline

GIRLZ ROCK!

# When We Were Kids

Holly

Jacqueline talked to Holly, another *Girlz Rock!* author.

**Jacqueline** "Did you have birthday parties when you were younger?"

**Holly** "I had some great parties. I still do. You're never too old for a great birthday party. I had one only recently and there was …"

**Jacqueline** "Music?"

**Holly** "Yes, and …"

**Jacqueline** "Presents?"

**Holly** "Yes, and …"

**Jacqueline** "Ca …"

**Holly** "CAKE!"

**Jacqueline** "I was going to say that!"

**Holly** "Thought you might."

GIRLZROCK!

# What a Laugh!

**Q** What birthday party game do rabbits like to play?

**A** Musical Hares!

# GIRLZROCK!

Read about the fun that girls have in these GIRLZROCK! titles:

**Birthday Party Bedlam**

**Pony Club**

**Doubles Trouble**

**Soccer Crazy**

**Dance Fever**

**Minigolf Face-off**

**Trapeze Dreams**

**Two at the Zoo**

... and 20 more great titles to choose from!